MW01093815

Career As A Doctor

*What They Do, How to Become One, and
What the Future Holds!*

Brian Rogers

KidLit-O Books

www.kidlito.com

© 2013. All Rights Reserved.

Cover Image © drubig-photo - Fotolia.com

Table of Contents

About KidCaps

KidLit-O is an imprint of BookCaps™ that is just for kids! Each month BookCaps will be releasing several books in this exciting imprint. Visit are website or like us on Facebook to see more!

Two doctors speak with a sick patient[1]

---

[1] Image source:

Introduction

Ashlyn Julian was only a few weeks old when one day in June 2013 her parents had trouble waking her up in her crib. When Ashlyn finally opened her eyes, she started to scream in pain and to throw up everywhere. Her parents had no idea what was going on and only knew that something was terribly wrong, so they immediately took her to the emergency room. The doctors at the hospital found that little Ashlyn had a scary condition called a brain aneurysm, which is where an artery in the brain starts to fill up and expand with blood (like a water balloon). Brain aneurysms can hurt the other parts of the brain around them and often start to bleed out of control. Aneurysms are particularly dangerous in adults and are even worse in babies like Ashlyn. After transferring baby Ashlyn to a larger hospital that had trained doctors that could take better care of her, everyone tried to find a solution to save Ashlyn's life.

In most cases, when doctors discover a brain aneurysm they will perform a particular surgery where they actually open up the patient's skull and put a distinctive metal clip near the base of the aneurysm to cut off the blood supply (like tying a knot in a balloon) before removing the aneurysm. However, in baby Ashlyn's case, a surgery like that would just be too dangerous, so the doctors had to find another solution. Doctor Koji Ebersole, an endovascular neurosurgeon (a doctor that performs surgery on the arteries in the brain) worked with a team of doctors to find a way to save Ashlyn's life. They finally decided to insert a small tube called a catheter into Ashlyn's neck and then to push some powerful glue through the tube all the way to the artery in her brain, and thus seal the hole that was causing the aneurysm. After a tremendously tense few hours of surgery, the aneurysm was fixed, and the pain in baby Ashlyn's head went away. By the next day, she could breathe normally on her own and soon went back home with her mom and dad, who were thankful for the hard work of the doctors.

Doctor Ebersole and his team were given an impossible situation, but they were able to figure out a solution that had never been seen before and use it to help baby Ashlyn. Their training, their quick thinking, their knowledge, and their desire to help the patient all came together and gave this story a truly happy ending. Would you have liked to have been on this team of doctors that helped the Julian family and saved baby Ashlyn's life? Can you imagine how thankful this family will be as they watch their little girl grow up and get stronger year by year, knowing that she might have died if it wasn't for those doctors?

Doctors are among the most respected members of society today. When was the last time that you visited a doctor? Sometimes we go to the doctor when we have a specific problem or when there is an emergency, and sometimes we just go for a checkup to make sure that everything is okay. Doctors help us to stay healthy, and they help us get better when we are sick. But have you ever thought about becoming a doctor yourself? Can you imagine how it would feel to spend your life helping others out when they most need it?

In the United States, there are almost 700,000 doctors who work hard to take care of their patients. Each doctor needs to have special qualities to be successful. What kinds of qualities? Experienced doctors have said that the ideal medical professional should have a real love for learning, a continued curiosity about medicine and medical techniques, and a real desire to help others in their time of need, no matter who that person is.

We can be thankful that there are people who have those qualities and who have decided to become doctors. None of us would ever want to live in a world where there weren't any doctors. After all, what would everyone do when they got sick or when they had a medical emergency?

Since the very beginning of human civilization, there have always been people who tried to make us feel better when we were sick. The ancient Egyptians learned the basics of human anatomy and about how to diagnose (determine) different kinds of diseases. The ancient Babylonians discovered how to treat specific diseases with therapies and medicines. The ancient Indians worked with herbs and different types of surgery. The ancient Greeks discovered how to more accurately identify diseases and injuries, including problems with patients' hearts and lungs.

Today, doctors continue to try and learn more about the human body and the different problems that people may have. But did you know that there aren't enough doctors in the United States today to treat all of the patients that are sick and that even more doctors will be needed in the future? Do you think that you can be one of the people who will help to fill that need? Do you have what it takes to be one of those who will continue the legacy of doctors throughout the centuries?

In this handbook, we will be talking about what a career as a doctor is all about. After reading it, you will have a good idea of the ups and downs of being a doctor and whether or not it is the career for you. What can you expect to learn? We will look at the career of a doctor in seven different sections. First, we will learn more about what doctors do. Did you know that there are many types of doctors and that some have received extra training to treat certain types of diseases? Do you know how much money a doctor makes each year? We will find out in the first section.

The second section will tell us what the training to be a doctor is like. While everybody knows that doctors make a lot of money, not everyone knows how expensive medical school is. We will talk about how long doctors must go to school and receive specific training and whether or not they ever stop learning.

The third section will answer the question: "Is being a doctor an easy job?" While you may think that doctors don't work as hard as construction workers or farmers, doctors have a tough job in other ways. This section will tell us why being a doctor can be difficult at times.

The fourth section will let us go along with a doctor on an average day. We will see as they talk to patients, do research, look at test results, and prescribe treatments. Do you know how many hours a day some doctors work? We will find out in this section.

The fifth section will tell us what the hardest part of being a doctor is. Although every job has its good parts and bad parts, doctors have to worry about life and death every day that they go to work. The decisions that they make can affect lots of people. This section will take a moment to tell us a little more about the challenges that affect many doctors.

Then the sixth section will show us what the future holds for doctors. In ten years, right about the time that you may decide to medical school, what kinds of exciting new technologies might doctors be using? Will there be lots of jobs available? We will talk about all this in the sixth section.

Finally, the seventh section will give you some idea of how you can get ready right now to become a doctor. Although doctors have to spend many years at school learning to practice medicine, there are several things that you can do even before you go to college that can help you on your way to becoming a doctor. We will talk about how you can get started now on the path to becoming a doctor.

Are you ready to learn more about this important and exciting career? Then let's start with the first section.

Chapter 1: What is a doctor?

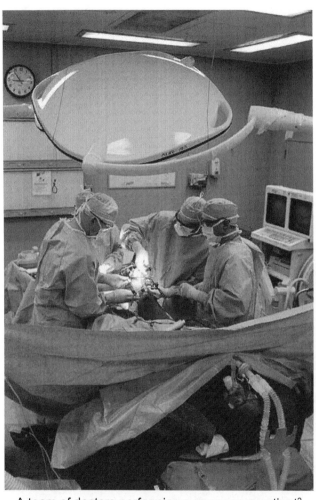

A team of doctors performing surgery on a patient[2]

---

[2] Image source: http://commons.wikimedia.org/wlkl/File:US_Navy_100215-N-4995K-184_Navy_doctors_perform_surgery_aboard_USNS_Comfort.jpg

Generally speaking, a doctor is someone who helps sick people to feel better. You have probably visited many doctors during your lifetime, and each of them helped you feel better from a different sickness or injury. But did you know that not all doctors are the same? Just like how some teachers teach more than one subject at school while others specialize in teaching just one subject (like history or math), different doctors work with different kinds of illnesses and diseases. Let's talk generally about what kinds of doctors there are, where they work, and what kind of money they make each year.

First off, all doctors share something in common-they all treat patients. The process starts when they listen to the patient describe the symptoms (specific pain or conditions caused by an illness or injury) that they are experiencing. The patient might describe feeling tired, sad, or something else. Then, the doctor must use their knowledge and experience to diagnose the problem right away or to do specific research and tests to decide what is going on with the patient's health. Then the doctor will prescribe a treatment, which may involve therapy, medicine, or surgery (or a combination of all three) to help the patient to feel better.

When you think of a doctor, most likely you are thinking of a General Practitioner. A doctor who is a General Practitioner must be ready to see patients who come in to their office with a wide range of problems. The patients may be suffering something as simple as a cold or as complicated as cancer. The General Practitioner must find out if it is something simple that can be treated quickly or if the patient should visit a second doctor (called a specialist) who can follow up on their condition.

A specialist is a doctor who, like some teachers at your school, focuses on one specific subject. There are many kinds of doctors who are specialists, and each one has a hugely important job to do when a person is sick. Would you like to learn about some of them? Here is a list of some of the more common specialties that some doctors learn and what kind of medicine they focus on.

Dermatology: A dermatologist focuses on skin problems, including skin cancer

General Surgery: A general surgeon can perform surgery on different areas of the body

Neurological Surgery: A neurological surgeon performs complex operations on a patient's brain

Pediatrics: A pediatric doctor focuses on helping young children who get sick

Radiation Oncology: A radiation oncologist uses special therapies to help patients with cancer

Urology: An urologist helps patients who have problems with their kidneys or bladder

Of course, there are many other specialties, but this list includes some of the most common ones. The next section will show us the education and training required to become a specialist, but in the meantime you can be sure that it involves years of studying and practice and learning from older, more experienced doctors while working in hospitals and clinics.

Most doctors begin by working in a large public or private hospital. After they have finished their training and get their medical license, they can apply for a job anywhere that they want and start trying to earn a good reputation by treating their patients well and by giving everyone they work with quality care. After several years of working in a hospital, some doctors choose to open their own office for medical treatment, something called a private practice. Many doctors will continue to work at a hospital, in addition to their private practice, which means that they are busy all week long helping lots of people.

In the United States, being a doctor usually means making a lot of money. The medical profession is among the highest paid professions in the country. How much money do doctors make each year? A general practitioner (a doctor that treats all sorts of basic problems) makes around $220,000 per year, while a doctor that practices a specialty can expect to earn closer to $396,000 or more each year. That's a lot of money!

Doctors the world over are respected for their knowledge, their abilities, and their warm desire to genuinely help other people to feel better and to enjoy their lives the best they can. Doctors help us when we are sick and heal us when we are injured. We can be extremely grateful that these wise men and women have chosen to spend their days helping others.

Chapter 2: What is the Training Like to Be a Doctor?

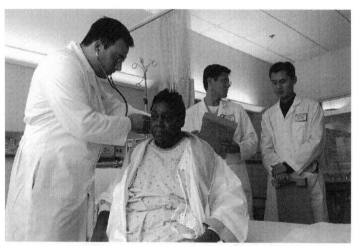

Younger doctors learn from more experienced doctors during their residency[3]

In the introduction, we saw the amazing work of the team of doctors that was able to help baby

[3] Image source: http://commons.wikimedia.org/wiki/File:Doctor_examines_patient.jpg

Ashlyn with a difficult problem. When the standard ways of treating her specific problem (a brain aneurysm) wouldn't work, the doctors had to think quickly to come up with an alternative idea that would save the patient's life. How were they able to solve that difficult situation so quickly? The answer has to do with the excellent training that each doctor on the team received.

How long do you think that a person has to study before they can begin to practice medicine? In other jobs, a new employee might be trained only for a few hours, and they only have to go to a few meetings or classroom sessions before they can start working. Doctors, on the other hand, have to deal with the lives of other people every day. Because so much is expected of them, doctors must receive lots of training. In the United States, a person must be trained for at least eleven years, and in some cases for up to fifteen years, before they can practice medicine on their own.

How is the training organized?

The first stage of training to become a doctor involves getting a bachelor's degree from the college of their choice. Normally, a student must study for four years to get a Bachelor's Degree. During these four years, the student studies subjects like biology, chemistry, math, English, and physics. Each class has difficult tests at least twice per year that the student needs to pass in order to get their degree.

After graduating from college, students will then apply to one of several medical schools that are spread across the country. There are two types of medical schools: one gives out a M.D. degree (Doctor of Medicine) and the other gives out a D.O. degree (Doctor of Osteopathy). Both treat patients and prescribe treatments and medicine, but D.O. doctors also focus on manipulating the bones of the skeletal system to find and treat problems.

The competition to get accepted at medical schools is intensely fierce, and some of the best schools only accept 2-4% of the students who apply. However, that number is not as severe as it seems, because most students apply to more than one school at a time. But what is medical school like for those who get accepted?

Medical school lasts for four years in most states. The first two years are spent mainly in the classroom and in laboratories, where the students expand on their knowledge and see how what they learned in college applies specifically to being a doctor. A lot of time is also spent on teaching the students how to communicate well and how to ask patients the right questions, questions that will give the doctor the information they need to help the person feel better.

The second two years of medical school are a little more hands-on, and the students (called "interns") spend much of their time as part of a medical team that visits actual patients in a real health care facility. They listen to the patients describe what they are feeling, and as a group they determine what the cause is and then recommend a treatment. The medical team (made up of resident doctors and interns) works under the supervision of a senior attending doctor with a lot of experience.

If the student does well on all of their assignments, then they will be able to graduate from medical school with a degree as either a M.D. or a D.O. Once the student has finished their formal education (eight years by this point) does that mean that they can run out and start treating any sick patients that they come across? Not yet.

Even though the students who graduate with their M.D. or D.O. have a great deal of knowledge and have received some training as part of a group, they are not yet ready to practice medicine alone. For the next three to eight years (depending on the specialty), each recently graduated doctor must work as a "resident doctor" in a hospital. Although they will be allowed to see patients one on one, they will still be closely supervised by a senior doctor. The more experienced doctor will help the younger doctor with any difficult cases that they must treat and will make sure that the doctor is applying everything that he or she has learned. During their residency, doctors must work exceptionally long hours (up to 80 hours per week) and often must stay at the hospital for more than 24 hours in a row without going home.

At the end of their residency period, a doctor will take a special three part test prepared by the United States Medical Licensing Examination

(USMLE). The tests are a mix of written information and interactions with patients, all of which which are observed by members of the USMLE. If the doctor does well on their tests, the USMLE will officially certify them and give them a license to practice medicine in the field that they studied for, which means that the doctor may now apply for a job anywhere in that state or may open up a private practice nearby.

Does that mean that the doctor is done learning? Not at all. Being a doctor means accepting a lifetime of learning. Doctors subscribe to medical journals that talk about new discoveries and techniques for treating patients. New technologies make doctors more effective- but doctors must learn how the new technology works and when to use it. Pharmaceutical companies make new medicines to treat diseases, and the doctor must constantly learn about each new medicine available for their specialty if they want to give their patients the best care possible.

After anywhere from eleven to fifteen years of studying and training, doctors can begin to practice medicine on their own. For the rest of their lives, they will continue to build on the foundation that they laid during those important first years.

Chapter 3: Is Being a Doctor An Easy Job?

A group of doctors at their job[4]

After what you have seen so far, you would probably agree that training to become a doctor is extremely difficult. A lot of time and money is spent studying; the average doctor graduates with over $200,000 in debt that must be paid to the different schools that he or she attended. But once they start to practice medicine, whether at

[4] Image source: http://tinyurl.com/kyme2do

a hospital, at a private practice, or both- is being a doctor an easy job? Have a look at the following information and answer that question for yourself.

Doctors have a very serious responsibility every time that they get dressed and go to work- they are dealing with the lives of other human beings. The decisions that they make will directly affect other people and can either make them feel better or worse. If a doctor makes a terribly bad decision they could even kill the patient that they are trying to save. Can you imagine walking around with that kind of responsibility on your shoulders?

A lot of doctors love what they do, but they aren't always as happy with the environment that they have to work in. Did you know that doctors often have problems with bureaucracy? Have you heard that word before? "Bureaucracy" refers to the problems that come from working within a large organization. In hospitals, where sometimes hundreds or even thousands of patients are treated each week, the doctors must stay organized to make sure that they work effectively. Experienced doctors are put in charge of departments and are overseen by the hospital administration. However, the doctors, nurses, and hospital administration don't always all agree on the best way to do things. While doctors may be more concerned with trying to help their patients, hospital administrators might be more concerned with trying to spend less money and treat more people. Often, doctors feel that they could do more good but that they are limited by the people in charge.

This often leads to another problem: too many patients. Because of the rules in some hospitals and because of the high cost and demands of medical school, there are not enough doctors in the United States. Often, one single doctor is required to see a large number of patients every day, which means that they end up spending less time talking to, listening, and thinking about each patient. Doctors sometimes feel pressured to diagnose a patient's problem more quickly than they would like to do. As a result, some doctors worry that spending such little time with each patient might lead to their making mistakes and missing important clues as to what is really going on. And many patients feel frustrated when they think that their doctor doesn't have enough time for them.

Do you remember how we saw earlier that medical students must study English when they are in college? Did that surprise you? Actually, one of the most important parts of being a doctor is communicating well. Doctors have to be able to explain complicated diseases and treatments to all kinds of patients, even those who are older or who have little education. In fact, helping a patient to understand what the problem is and what they need to do to make it better can be one of the hardest parts of a doctor's job.

Doctors face all kinds of challenges each and every time that they go to work. Although some of them are harder than others, you would probably agree that being a doctor is not an easy job.

Chapter 4: What Is An Average Day Like for a Doctor?

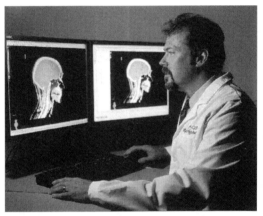

A doctor looks at some test results to help a sick patient[5]

All doctors follow the same basic routine each day: see patients, learn about the each patient's medical history, prescribe certain tests, diagnose the problem, and then recommend (and possibly

[5] Image source: http://commons.wikimedia.org/wiki/File:Doctor_review_brain_images.jpg

carry out) a treatment. Let's look a little closer at each of these activities to try to understand the valuable work of doctors.

Seeing patients. Every doctor needs to meet personally with a patient before they can truly understand the best way to treat that patient. In some cases, the patient will walk in off the street to see a family doctor (a general practitioner) while, in other cases, the patient will be sent to see a specialist after visiting their family doctor. Either way, the doctor will ask the patient a series of questions to find out more about what is happening. They might ask what medicines the patient is taking, if they have had any injuries in the past, and what specifically they are feeling. Then the patient must, in as much detail as they can, explain exactly what is going on. The more information that a patient gives, the more helpful a doctor can be.

Learning about the medical history. Sometimes this step happens during the initial visit with the patient and sometimes it happens a little later. Either way, it is particularly important for the doctor to know as much as they can about the patient that they are treating. Detailed records are kept in a special file in the doctor's office that explain past illnesses and treatments, as well as basic information like the height, weight, age, and overall health of the patient. When a family doctor sends a patient to a specialist, they will often send a copy of this medical history to help the specialist treat the patient.

Prescribing tests. Doctors want to find out as much as they can about the patient's body before they recommend any certain treatment. A terribly helpful way to get information is to recommend certain tests. Each case is different, but a doctor might recommend X-rays, ultrasounds, blood work, urine or stool samples, a MRI (Magnetic Resonance Imaging) or even a tissue sample of some affected part of the body. These tests will usually be carried out and performed by technicians in a laboratory who will prepare a report telling the doctor what they have found.

Diagnosing the problem. After meeting the patient, learning about their medical history, and getting the results back from the different tests, a doctor is now ready to diagnose the problem. Using the knowledge and experience that they have, many problems are relatively easy to identify. However, sometimes an extremely difficult disease or condition shows up, and the doctor must spend long hours researching, thinking, and speaking with fellow physicians about what might be going on. Once a doctor (or team of doctors) has figured out the problem, then they can recommend a solution.

Recommending a treatment. After the disease or cause of illness has been identified, doctors can then take the next step and prescribe a solution (a treatment) to help the patient feel better. In some cases, it may be as simple as telling the patient to take a certain medicine for a while, while, in other cases, the solution may be more complicated and involve one or more surgeries. In the case of surgery, the patient may be recommended to another surgeon or the doctor themself (if they are properly trained) might perform the surgery.

Doctors must use good judgment each step of the way. Although some patients might wish that the whole process was a little bit faster, they should be glad that the doctors don't want to rush their decision or treatment. When they finally decide how to help the patient, they want it to be after much research, investigation, and thought.

In some cases, doctors may have to repeat this process several times in order to correctly diagnose a particularly difficult disease. Some illnesses have similar symptoms and are difficult to tell apart, even after a lot of research. So it's a brilliant idea for sick individuals not to lose their patience when seeing a doctor, even if they can't right away see the results of all the visits.

Doctors work extremely long hours, especially those who spend time in hospitals. It is not uncommon for a surgeon or specialist to work 60 or more hours a week. Even though they are tired (and might miss their friends and families), doctors love helping people and so are willing to give of themselves in this special way. Shouldn't we be grateful to the doctors who help us so much?

Chapter 5: What Is the Hardest Part of Being a Doctor?

We have already seen some of the unique challenges that doctors have to deal with. Along with the awesome responsibility of caring for other people's lives, they also must keep educating themselves, deal with the bureaucracy at their jobs, and try to treat large numbers of patients without lowering the quality of care that they give each one of them. However, while each of those can be a real challenge, there are even harder parts of being a doctor. Let's look at two of them.

The first has to do with death. People see doctors when they aren't feeling well. In many cases, the problem is not too serious, and the doctor can help them quickly. In other cases, however, the problem is uncommonly serious and the doctor is limited in how much they can do.

Doctors are acutely aware of a sad reality of life-everybody dies. When we are young, it can be hard to think about people getting sick and dying. We normally think about grandparents dying and older neighbors, but we might think that our friends and we will live forever. Doctors know that everybody, even if they visit a doctor every single day of their life, will eventually get sick and die. The goal of doctors is to try to give people comfortable and long lives, but even physicians have their limitations.

Doctors learn to really love many of their patients, so imagine how much it hurts them to see their friends get weaker and weaker until they eventually stop breathing and die. While doctors know that they have done everything they could, some still feel a little bit of guilt, wondering if maybe there was some other treatment that might have worked better. In most cases, doctors will have done everything just right, but even so their strong emotions can sometimes get the better of them.

Some doctors also have the tough responsibility of telling family members when a patient has died. Can you imagine seeing a patient die during surgery and having to go out and tell the family that their beloved father, mother, husband, wife, or even child has died? Can you imagine watching them cry, or listening to them get angry at you for not saving the patient? In times of extreme emotion, some people act a little crazy and doctors have to be prepared to help them through those moments.

Doctors also have to worry about something called a "malpractice lawsuit". When a patient is not happy with the result of a doctor's treatment, they can take the doctor to court to ask for their money back and to try to make the doctor lose their license to practice medicine. While most doctors do an excellent job helping their patients to feel better, this arrangement makes sure that the few bad doctors can't hurt any more people in the future. But did you know that there are some people who make up lies to try to get money from a doctor?

As we saw earlier, doctors have extremely high salaries, and this makes them the target of all kinds of bad people. Some of them will invent stories that make a doctor look bad. Some will even fake injuries and illnesses! They will try to take the doctor to court to get money and to make the doctor lose their good reputation. Even if the bad person loses the case, the innocent doctor will still have lost money paying for a lawyer and will have spent long hours away from the job they love. As you can probably imagine, a lot of doctors are afraid that a patient of theirs might someday turn out to be a bad person who wants to start a malpractice lawsuit.

Dealing with death and worrying about malpractice lawsuits are two very real concerns for doctors across the country.

Chapter 6: What does the future hold for doctors?

A new technology is demonstrated at an important meeting[6]

One hundred years ago, doctors practiced medicine very differently. Although they were trying the best that they could, doctors were often limited by a lack of knowledge and by poor

[6] Image source: http://listverse.com/2013/03/22/10-medical-technologies-that-could-shape-the-future/

technology. However, the discovery of X-ray technology, better medicines, and cleaner hospitals has made it possible for doctors to give better care than ever before to their patients. What kinds of new technologies will be used in the future to help patients get better even faster? Let's look at a few of the exciting new ideas being worked on now.

1) <u>3D printers to build replacement bones.</u> Can you see the picture at the beginning of this section? What do you notice about the jawbone of the skull? The jawbone is made out of metal that was printed on a remarkable machine: a 3D printer. A 3D printer is a machine that can make just about any shape you can imagine by building layer upon layer of material. Doctors are hoping that, in the future, they can replace missing bones of patients using this new technology. But can it really work?

In June of 2011, an 83 year old woman suffered from a chronic bone infection and was unable to speak, chew her food, or swallow correctly. At her age, a new jawbone might be rejected by her body, so doctors decided to test out a 3D printed jawbone, made of titanium. The surgery went well, and within four days the patient was back home and living her life as before. The new technology worked, and doctors are confident that more and more patients will be able to benefit from 3D printed bones.

2) <u>Non-invasive surgery.</u> Do you remember the exciting case of baby Ashlyn from the introduction? When doctors discovered that she had a brain aneurysm, they weren't too sure about how to treat the problem. In adults, surgeons normally will open the head and cut out the aneurysm. But in the case of an infant, a surgery like that might kill her. So what was the solution?

The doctors decided to use a type of procedure called "non-invasive surgery". Instead of making a big cut and opening up the patient, this type of surgery uses small tools and tubes to help the patient. In baby Ashlyn's case, a small cut was made in a neck vein and the tools were put into a tube in the vein and then pushed to where the aneurysm was. The aneurysm was closed off and removed, and baby Ashlyn was able to recover completely.

When working with certain types of heart problems, doctors have learned that the patient often has less pain and recovers more quickly if they can use a similar method. For example, doctors replacing heart valves are now opening up a small hole in the leg of some patients and then pushing the tools all the way up the vein (through a small tube called a catheter) to the heart. Then they can replace the heart valve and remove the tools, all without causing a lot of pain to the patient or making them lose a lot of blood.

This way, instead of spending days in the hospital after a valve transplant, patients can often go home the next day. This type of surgery will continue to save lives in the future.

3) <u>Small cameras inside capsules.</u> When doctors are helping some people with problems in their digestive system, they need to see what is going on inside the patient. For years, the most common way to see inside the patient was to stick a camera either down their throat or up into their behind. As you can imagine, these tests, while very important, are quite uncomfortable for the patient. Is there an easier way for doctors to get the information they need without making the patient feel uncomfortable?

A new technology to help doctors[7]

A new capsule has been developed by a team of scientists and uses X-ray technology to make a sort of map of the inside of a patient's digestive system. After swallowing the capsule, the patient can go about their activities as normal, while the X-ray images are transmitted to a small device worn on the wrist of the patient. Then, during their next appointment, the doctor can download the images from the device and see if the patient has anything to be worried about. This device can save thousands of people each year who die

[7] Image source: http://nocamels.com/2012/06/will-tiny-screening-capsule-replace-colonoscopy/

from colon cancer, and it can make sure that the treatment is not painful or embarrassing.

The future of being a doctor will surely be exciting with all of these new technologies. However, will there still be enough jobs in the medical field? Absolutely. Right now, the US needs about 16,000 more doctors to start working, especially in rural areas far away from big cities. Within the next ten years or so, that number is expected to grow to over 130,000[8]. What are the reasons for the growing shortage?

Many of the people who are now working as doctors are simply getting older and will be retiring soon- and there aren't enough new doctors to replace them all. Combined with the fact that patients are living longer and longer, that means that, in the new few years, there will be even more patients for each doctor. That

[8] Info source: http://www.cnbc.com/id/100546118

means that anyone who graduates as a doctor in the future will not have any trouble finding a job.

And although it may sound a little strange to say it, humans will not stop getting sick anytime soon. We have needed doctors for thousands of years, and we will surely need them in the future. Even though technology will help doctors to treat patients better and to give them happier and longer lives, science is still a long ways of from completely curing all sicknesses and old age.

The future of medicine is secure as intelligent men and women continue to work to find new ways of helping people who don't feel well.

Chapter 7: How can you get ready now to become a doctor?

A young student learns about Chemistry[9]

The official path to being a doctor starts after a student has enrolled in college and has started to take the required courses. But is there anything that you can do right now to get ready for being a doctor? Absolutely. Let's look at a few goals you can try to reach right now, before you go to college.

---

[9] Image source: http://www.uta.edu/cos/cstudents.php

Doctors are expected to be good students all through college, medical school, and for the rest of their lives. But why wait until then to develop strong study habits? While you are still young, try to develop proficient reading and comprehension skills, turn in your homework on time, study well for tests, and ask about doing extra credit. The better your grades and study habits are, the better college and medical school you will get into, which can help you to become a better doctor.

Also, as we saw earlier, one of the keys to being a successful doctor has to do with having a real desire to help people. Doctors spend long hours at hospitals and must endure difficult conditions, all with the goal of helping their patients to feel better. So find ways now to help others. Whether you help your neighbors to do chores around the house or you volunteer in the community, seeing how great it feels to do something nice for another person can give you an idea of what doctors feel most of the time.

We have seen some of the real challenges that come with working in the medical field. Before some medical schools accept students, they like to see that the person is sure that being a doctor is what they want. Medical schools like to see students who have spent some time working in the medical profession. How can you do that? Many hospitals or doctor's offices are willing to train new employees to work in areas that don't directly involve patient care. You can get some real life experience by cleaning, filing papers, or transcribing medical files. Although the work may not be exciting, it will give you a front row seat to life as a doctor and will let you ask any questions you want to the physician.

College and medical school cost a lot of money, and not everyone's family is has saved up enough to pay for them. So what can you do to avoid having tons of debt when you graduate? Talk to your school counselor about scholarships and financial aid. These are special ways that you can get money from the government and from local organizations who want to help you reach your career goals. The prerequisites usually have to do with good grades, good conduct, and being active in the community.

We also saw how good doctors are defined by more than just their training- they also have important qualities like curiosity, a good work ethic, and a refusal to give up even when things are tough. They also have to make decisions even in moments of intense pressure. So why not start developing those important qualities now? Try to learn about all kinds of different subjects by going online, to the local library, and by watching documentaries. Learn to value hard work and don't try to get out of doing your chores. Work hard to do a good job on your homework and school projects, and don't quit just because things look tough.

To get ready for your formal education as a pre-med student at college and later at medical school, find out now what kinds of classes you should be taking in middle and high school. Does the college that you want to attend require two language courses and four math courses? Then make sure that you are signed up for them. And what kind of entry requirements does the medical school have? Visit their website or call them to find out. You may even be able to get a brochure that will explain how you can get ready. That way, you won't have any problems applying and getting accepted.

Finally, being a doctor means knowing how to communicate with and get along with lots of different people, and sometimes it even means working as part of a team. Doctors have to choose their words carefully and make hard things easy to understand when they are speaking with parents. And when working with other doctors, especially during a surgery, they must work well as part of a team.

There are a lot of things that you can do right now to get ready to become a doctor.

Conclusion

A doctor hard at work[10]

This handbook has given us a great introduction to having a career as a doctor. Did you learn anything new? What was your favorite part? Let's have a quick review of some of the most important things that we learned in each section so that we don't forget them.

First, we learned more about what doctors do. Did you see how there are many types of

[10] Image source: http://tinyurl.com/kbm493r

doctors and that some have received extra training to treat certain types of diseases? We saw how both general practitioners and specialists train for years to learn how to make sick people feel better. Whether they work in large hospitals or private practices (or even at both), doctors work hard at their jobs. And they make a lot of money for their hard work. Did you see how much money a doctor makes each year? Doctors make between $200,000 to $400,000 per year! Of course, they need that money in the beginning to pay off all of their student loans!

The second section told us what the training to be a doctor is like. Do you remember some of the facts that we learned about the training required to become a doctor? We saw that, after attending college and getting a Bachelor's in Science degree, doctors must attend medical school for four years and then receive close training as residents for another three to eight years, depending on their specialty. That's a lot of schooling and training! But we also saw how doctors never truly stop learning and how they always try to stay up-to-date with the newest technologies, discoveries, and medicines so that they can give their patients the best treatment possible.

The third section answered the question: "Is being a doctor an easy job?" While you may think that doctors don't work as hard as construction workers or farmers, we saw that doctors have a tough job in other ways. Do you remember some of the unique challenges that doctors have to deal with on a daily basis? Apart from their intensive training and continuing education, doctors have to live with the pressure that comes with caring for the lives of other people. They know that the decisions they make and the words that they choose can make a real difference for their patients. Doctors must also deal with bureaucratic problems at the hospitals they work at and the must find ways of giving good care to high numbers of patients. In fact, there are too many patients for the amount of doctors today, which means that doctors feel a lot of pressure to spend less time with each person.

The fourth section let us go along with a doctor on an average day at their job. We were able to see the basic routines of doctors all across the country. After speaking with the patient and finding out a little bit about the symptoms that they have, doctors will learn a little bit more about the medical history of the person before sending the patient to a laboratory to get some specific tests done on their body. Once the doctor has all the information in front of them, they will try and decide what the patient's health problem is. Then, they will recommend a specific treatment. All doctors follow this basic method to treat patients, and they may treat many patients in just one day.

The fifth section told us what the hardest part of being a doctor is. Although every job has good parts and bad parts, doctors have to worry about life and death each day that they go to work. The decisions that they make can affect lots of people. We saw how dealing with death is a very real and a very sad part of being a doctor. We also saw how some doctors worry about bad people trying to take them to court for malpractice and how that might affect their reputation.

Then the sixth section showed us what the future holds for doctors. In ten years, right about the time that you may decide to medical school, what kinds of exciting new technologies might doctors be using? Will there be lots of jobs available? We saw some of the new inventions that will help doctors to give better and better care to their patients. 3D printers can replace bones in patients with infections, cancer, or serious injuries, while new capsules can reveal problems inside the digestive track of patients. We also saw a new method of surgery (called non-invasive surgery) that minimizes the pain and recuperation time of the people who receive it. These new ideas and others like them will continue make medicine safer and more effective in the future. We also saw how more and more doctors will be needed in the future to help all the people who will get sick.

Finally, the seventh section will gave you some ideas of how you can ready now to become a doctor. Although doctors have to spend many years at school learning to practice medicine, there are several things that you can do even before you go to college that can help you to become a doctor. Do you remember what suggestions you saw? Are there any of them that you are going to try and put into practice? Along with the basics (develop good study habits), we saw how it would be a good idea for you to start helping people in your community and to get some practice working in the medical field. Talking to your school counselor about financial aid and college entrance requirements can help you to save time and money when going to college later on. And do your homework to find out what kind of people get accepted to the medical school that you want to attend. That way, you can increase your chances of getting accepted and becoming a doctor.

Doctors are hugely important people, and we can't possibly imagine what our lives would be like if we didn't have them with us. They help us to feel better when we are sick, and they give us reliable advice when we need it most. After reading this handbook, do you think that the career of a doctor is the right one for you? Then don't waste any time getting ready for this exciting career! Learn as much as you can and talk to as many doctors as you can. Then you too can help to save lives of patients.

33273293R00039

Made in the USA
Lexington, KY
20 June 2014